by Iain Gray

Lang**Syne**
PUBLISHING
WRITING *to* REMEMBER

79 Main Street, Newtongrange,
Midlothian EH22 4NA
Tel: 0131 344 0414   Fax: 0845 075 6085
E-mail: info@lang-syne.co.uk
www.langsyneshop.co.uk

Design by Dorothy Meikle
Printed by Ricoh Print Scotland
© Lang Syne Publishers Ltd 2015

All rights reserved. No part of this publication may be reproduced, stored
or introduced into a retrieval system, or transmitted in any form or by any
means (electronic, mechanical, photocopying, recording or otherwise) without
the prior written permission of Lang Syne Publishers Ltd.

ISBN 978-1-85217-581-8

Bell

MOTTO:
I love fervently.

CREST:
A falcon.

NAME variations include:
Beal
Beale
Beall
Belle

Chapter one:

The origins of popular surnames

by George Forbes and Iain Gray

If you don't know where you came from, you won't know where you're going is a frequently quoted observation and one that has a particular resonance today when there has been a marked upsurge in interest in genealogy, with increasing numbers of people curious to trace their family roots.

Main sources for genealogical research include census returns and official records of births, marriages and deaths – and the key to unlocking the detail they contain is obviously a family surname, one that has been 'inherited' and passed from generation to generation.

No matter our station in life, we all have a surname – but it was not until about the middle of the fourteenth century that the practice of being identified by a particular surname became commonly established throughout the British Isles.

Previous to this, it was normal for a person to be identified through the use of only a forename.

But as population gradually increased and there were many more people with the same forename, surnames were adopted to distinguish one person, or community, from another.

Many common English surnames are patronymic in origin, meaning they stem from the forename of one's father – with 'Johnson,' for example, indicating 'son of John.'

It was the Normans, in the wake of their eleventh century conquest of Anglo-Saxon England, a pivotal moment in the nation's history, who first brought surnames into usage – although it was a gradual process.

For the Normans, these were names initially based on the title of their estates, local villages and chateaux in France to distinguish and identify these landholdings.

Such grand descriptions also helped enhance the prestige of these warlords and generally glorify their lofty positions high above the humble serfs slaving away below in the pecking order who had only single names, often with Biblical connotations as in Pierre and Jacques.

The only descriptive distinctions among the peasantry concerned their occupations, like 'Pierre the swineherd' or 'Jacques the ferryman.'

Roots of surnames that came into usage in England not only included Norman-French, but also Old French, Old Norse, Old English, Middle English, German, Latin, Greek, Hebrew and the Gaelic languages of the Celts.

The Normans themselves were originally Vikings, or 'Northmen', who raided, colonised and eventually settled down around the French coastline.

The had sailed up the Seine in their longboats in 900AD under their ferocious leader Rollo and ruled the roost in north eastern France before sailing over to conquer England in 1066 under Duke William of Normandy – better known to posterity as William the Conqueror, or King William I of England.

Granted lands in the newly-conquered England, some of their descendants later acquired territories in Wales, Scotland and Ireland – taking not only their own surnames, but also the practice of adopting a surname, with them.

But it was in England where Norman rule and custom first impacted, particularly in relation to the adoption of surnames.

8   *The origins of popular surnames*

This is reflected in the famous *Domesday Book*, a massive survey of much of England and Wales, ordered by William I, to determine who owned what, what it was worth and therefore how much they were liable to pay in taxes to the voracious Royal Exchequer.

Completed in 1086 and now held in the National Archives in Kew, London, 'Domesday' was an Old English word meaning 'Day of Judgement.'

This was because, in the words of one contemporary chronicler, "its decisions, like those of the Last Judgement, are unalterable."

It had been a requirement of all those English landholders – from the richest to the poorest – that they identify themselves for the purposes of the survey and for future reference by means of a surname.

This is why the *Domesday Book*, although written in Latin as was the practice for several centuries with both civic and ecclesiastical records, is an invaluable source for the early appearance of a wide range of English surnames.

Several of these names were coined in connection with occupations.

These include Baker and Smith, while Cooks, Chamberlains, Constables and Porters were

Bell 9

to be found carrying out duties in large medieval households.

The church's influence can be found in names such as Bishop, Friar and Monk while the popular name of Bennett derives from the late fifth to mid-sixth century Saint Benedict, founder of the Benedictine order of monks.

The early medical profession is represented by Barber, while businessmen produced names that include Merchant and Sellers.

Down at the village watermill, the names that cropped up included Millar/Miller, Walker and Fuller, while other self-explanatory trades included Cooper, Tailor, Mason and Wright.

Even the scenery was utilised as in Moor, Hill, Wood and Forrest – while the hunt and the chase supplied names that include Hunter, Falconer, Fowler and Fox.

Colours are also a source of popular surnames, as in Black, Brown, Gray/Grey, Green and White, and would have denoted the colour of the clothing the person habitually wore or, apart from the obvious exception of 'Green', one's hair colouring or even complexion.

The surname Red developed into Reid, while

Blue was rare and no-one wanted to be associated with yellow.

Rather self-important individuals took surnames that include Goodman and Wiseman, while physical attributes crept into surnames such as Small and Little.

Many families proudly boast the heraldic device known as a Coat of Arms, as featured on our front cover.

The central motif of the Coat of Arms would originally have been what was borne on the shield of a warrior to distinguish himself from others on the battlefield.

Not featured on the Coat of Arms, but high-lighted on page three, is the family motto and related crest – with the latter frequently different from the central motif.

Adding further variety to the rich cultural heritage that is represented by surnames is the appearance in recent times in lists of the 100 most common names found in England of ones that include Khan, Patel and Singh – names that have proud roots in the vast sub-continent of India.

Echoes of a far distant past can still be found in our surnames and they can be borne with pride in commemoration of our forebears.

Chapter two:

On the borderline

Present in the British Isles from the earliest times, 'Bell' is a surname with a number of possible points of origin.

As an occupational name, it would have referred to a bell maker or bell ringer, while as a topographical, or locational name, it may have referred to someone who lived near a bell tower – a prominent feature of the landscape.

Rather more romantically, it also derives from the Old French 'bel', or 'beau', indicating 'fair' or 'handsome', while its Scots-Gaelic form is *Mac Giolla Mhaoil*, meaning 'son of the servant of the devotee.'

The name appears early in the historical record of England, with Ailuuardus filius Bell listed in the *Domesday Book*, in Suffolk, in 1086, and a Hugo Bel recorded in Hampshire in 1148.

But the name is particularly identified with the north of England, specifically the area of the small village of Gilsland, located near Hadrian's Wall, and an unusual village in that part of it lies in Northumberland and part in Cumbria.

Across the border with Scotland there was another family, or clan, of Bells, known as the Bells of Middlebie, in Dumfriesshire, and referred to by some sources as 'cousins' of the Bells of Gilsland.

These families may indeed have been related, albeit distantly, and descended from a Norman follower of the Scottish monarch David I, who reigned from 1124 to 1153, and who settled in the Borders area at the invitation of David, impressed as he was with Norman customs and manners.

Both the Bells of Gilsland and the Bells of Middlebie were among those families regarded as Border reivers – who took their name from their lawless custom of reiving, or raiding, not only their neighbours' livestock, but also that of their neighbours across the border.

The word 'bereaved', for example, indicating to have suffered loss, derives from the original 'reived', meaning to have suffered loss of property.

A Privy Council report of 1608 graphically described how the 'wild incests, adulteries, convocation of the lieges, shooting and wearing of hackbuts, pistols, lances, daily bloodshed, oppression, and disobedience in civil matters, neither are nor has been punished.'

Bell 13

A constant thorn in the flesh of both the English and Scottish authorities was the cross-border raiding and pillaging carried out by well-mounted and heavily armed men, the contingent from the Scottish side of the border known and feared as 'moss troopers.'

It was in an attempt to bring order to what was known as the wild 'debateable land' on both sides of the border, that Alexander II of Scotland signed the Treaty of York in 1237, which established for the first time the border between the two nations as a line running from the Solway to the Tweed.

On either side of the border there were three 'marches' or areas of administration, the West, East, and Middle Marches, and a warden governed these.

Complaints from either side of the border were dealt with on Truce days, when the wardens of the different marches would act as arbitrators. There was also a law known as the Hot Trod, that granted anyone who had their livestock stolen the right to pursue the thieves and recover their property.

While many of the Border Bells gained notoriety as reivers, others of the name were engaged in rather more peaceful pursuits.

Born in Norfolk in the early years of the sixteenth century, Sir Robert Bell served as Speaker of

14 *On the borderline*

the House of Commons from 1572 until a year before his death in 1577, during the reign of Elizabeth I.

In addition to his trusted post of Speaker, he also held other positions that included Commissioner of Grain and Chief Baron of the Exchequer.

In early twentieth century politics, Richard Bell, along with the Scottish socialist Keir Hardie, was one of the first two Labour Members of Parliament.

Born in 1859 in Merthyr Tydfil and general secretary for a time of the Amalgamated Society of Railway Servants, he entered the House of Commons as MP for Derby in 1900; he died in 1930.

In more turbulent times, Arthur Bell was a Roman Catholic martyr during the English Civil War.

King Charles I had incurred the wrath of Parliament by his insistence on the 'divine right' of monarchs, and added to this was Parliament's fear of Catholic 'subversion' against the state and the king's stubborn refusal to grant demands for religious and constitutional concessions.

Matters came to a head with the outbreak of the civil war in 1642, with Parliamentary forces, known as the New Model Army and commanded by Oliver Cromwell and Sir Thomas Fairfax, arrayed against the Royalist army of the king.

Bell 15

In what became an increasingly bloody and complex conflict, spreading to Scotland and Ireland and with rapidly shifting loyalties on both sides, the king was eventually captured and executed in January of 1649 on the orders of Parliament.

Born at Temple-Broughton, near Worcester, in 1590, Arthur Bell was aged 28 when he entered the Franciscan Order at Segovia, Spain.

Ministering for a time as a Franciscan priest in Scotland, he returned to his native England in 1637. Six years later, amid the anti-Royalist and anti-Catholic hysteria of the time, he was arrested by Parliamentary troops at Stevenage, Hertfordshire, on suspicion of being a spy.

A search of his papers revealed he was a priest – a capital offence at the time – and, confined for a time in London's Newgate prison, he was later sentenced to the horrific ordeal of being hanged, drawn and quartered.

It is said that when the grim sentence was passed he thanked his judges 'for the favour they were conferring on him in allowing him to die for Christ.'

He was beatified as The Blessed Arthur Bell by Pope John Paul II in November of 1987, along with other martyrs to the Catholic faith.

16 *On the borderline*

Bearers of the Bell name have gained high honours and distinction, with four baronetcies created in the Baronetage of the United Kingdom.

The Bell Baronetcy of Rounton Grange, in the County of Washington Hall in the County of Durham, was created in 1885 for the Liberal politician and immensely wealthy ironmaster Lowthian Bell.

In 1895, the Bell Baronetcy of Marlborough Terrace was created for James Bell, who served as Lord Provost of Glasgow from 1892 to 1896, while the Bell Baronetcy of Framewood, in the County of Buckingham, was created in 1908 for John Charles Bell, Lord Mayor of London from 1907 to 1908.

In 1909, the Bell Baronetcy of Mynthurst, in the County of Suffolk, was created for Henry Bell.

Meanwhile, the recognised Coat of Arms for English bearers of the Bell name features the crest of a falcon and motto *I love fervently*, while the Coat of Arms for the Scottish clan features the crest of a hand grasping a dagger and motto *I beir (bear) the bel (bell)*.

Bell

Chapter three:

Inventive genius

Bearers of the proud name of Bell have stamped a memorable mark on the historical record through their pioneering work in medicine, engineering and the sciences.

One famous family of Bells is one that included the Scottish anatomist and surgeon John Bell.

Born in Edinburgh in 1763 and, along with John Hunter and Pierre-Joseph Desault considered one of the founders of the modern surgery of the vascular system, he lectured in his native city in addition to practising for a time as a surgeon in the Royal Infirmary.

Responsible for important works that include his 1801 *Principles of Surgery* and *Anatomy of the Human Body*, he died in 1820.

He was an older brother of the anatomist, surgeon, neurologist and prolific writer on theological matters Sir Charles Bell.

Born in Edinburgh in 1774, his early surgical training was conducted as an assistant to his brother John.

18 *Inventive genius*

A member of the Royal College of Surgeons in Edinburgh he also became, in 1824, the first professor of anatomy and surgery at the College of Surgeons, London; a Fellow of both the Royal Society of Edinburgh and the Royal Society of London, he died in 1842.

Another brother was George Joseph Bell, the noted advocate born in 1770 and who died in 1820.

The pioneer of the development of the steamship, Henry Bell was the Scottish engineer born in 1767 at Torpichen, near Bathgate, West Lothian.

From a family of builders, engineers and millwrights, he was apprenticed as a stonemason and then, in 1783, as a millwright.

Later studying ship modelling it was in 1812, having moved to the Scottish west coast town of Helensburgh, that he built his famed steamboat the *Comet* – constructed at Port Glasgow and named after a comet that had been visible in the heavens for a number of months during 1811 to 1812.

In August of 1812 he launched a passenger service on the *Comet* – the first successful one of its kind in Europe – plying between Glasgow, Greenock and Helensburgh.

Despite his invention of steam-powered

Bell

19

vessels becoming universally adopted in his lifetime, poor management of his finances meant that he spent his later years in great poverty.

He died in 1830, while there is an obelisk to his memory on the rock of Dunglass, the promontory on the Clyde located just over two miles above Dumbarton.

Returning to the world of medicine, Joseph Bell was the surgeon recognised as having been the main inspiration for Sir Arthur Conan Doyle's famous fictional sleuth Sherlock Holmes.

Born in 1837, it was while Bell was a lecturer at the medical school of Edinburgh University that Doyle attended his classes, later serving as his clerk at the city's Royal Infirmary.

A pioneer in the field of forensic science, or forensic pathology, he was famed for his uncanny powers of deduction – a gift shared by Sherlock Holmes; a Fellow of the Royal College of Surgeons of Edinburgh and surgeon to Queen Victoria when she visited Scotland, he died in 1911.

Another noted family of Bells is one that included Alexander Melville Bell, the pioneer of phonetics born in Edinburgh in 1819.

A lecturer on speech elocution at Edinburgh University, he later moved to North America, where he lectured on philology at Queen's College, in Kingston, Ontario and in Washington D.C.

Devoting himself to the education of the deaf, he developed the technique known as Visible Speech – in which alphabetical characters are represented by graphic diagrams showing the various positions and motions of the lips, tongue and mouth.

A Fellow of the Royal Scottish Society of Arts, the Educational Institute of Scotland and the American Association for the Advancement of Science, he died in 1905.

Through his marriage to Eliza Grace Symonds, daughter of a British naval surgeon, he was the father of the engineer and scientist Alexander Graham Bell, recognised as the inventor of the first practical telephone.

Born in Edinburgh in 1847, it was after settling with his parents in North America when he was aged 23 that he dedicated his genius to intensive research on both hearing and speech.

As a pioneer in what became known as acoustic telegraphy, this culminated in his development of a device that utilised a liquid transmitter with a diaphragm that caused a needle to vibrate when the device was spoken into.

Bell 21

It was a basic forerunner of what we now know as that indispensable tool of modern communications, the telephone.

It was first tested on March 10, 1876, in his laboratory in Boston, when he used the device to speak his assistant, Thomas A. Watson, with the command: "Mr Watson, come here. I want to see you."

Watson, who had been listening at the receiving end of the device in an adjoining room, clearly heard the command.

Bell's U.S. patent for the telephone described it as "the method of, and apparatus for, transmitting vocal or other sounds telegraphically... by causing electrical undulations, similar in form to the vibrations of the air accompanying the said vocal or other sound."

He died in 1922, and while debate still continues to this day as to whether or not he may have utilised research carried out by the American inventor Elisha Gray, he has been accorded a number of honours.

The U.S. Post Office issued a commemorative stamp honouring him in 1940 as part of its *Famous Americans* series, while in 2002 he was ranked in a BBC nationwide poll as 57th in its *100 Greatest*

Britons list; he is also listed in the National Library of Scotland's *Scottish Science Hall of Fame*.

Keeping the spirit of inventive genius in the family, he was the uncle of the Irish scientist Chichester Alexander Bell.

The son of David Charles Bell, elder brother of Alexander Melville Bell, he was born in Dublin in 1848.

Qualified in not only chemistry but also in medicine and surgery, it was along with Alexander Graham Bell and his scientific colleague Charles Tainter that he was responsible for developing improved versions of the phonograph, forerunner of the record player – leading to the formation in 1886 of the Volta Graphaphone Company.

Awarded the prestigious John Scott Medal of the Franklin Institute in 1900, he died in 1924.

In more contemporary times, John Stewart Bell was the Northern Irish physicist who gives his name to *Bell's Theorem*, utilised in the highly complex study of quantum physics.

Born in Belfast in 1928, it was eighteen years after his death in 1990 that the University of Toronto's Centre for Quantum Information and Quantum Control created the John Stewart Bell Prize in his honour.

Bell 23

Chapter four:

On the world stage

An American actress known for box-office hits that include the 2010 *Frozen* and the 2011 *Final Destination 5*, Emma Jean Bell was born in 1986 in Woodstown, New Jersey.

Making her film debut in the 2007 *Gracie*, she has also appeared in television series that include *The Walking Dead*, *Supernatural*, *CSI: Miami* and *Law & Order*.

Best known for his character of Alf Ramsay in the early years of the Australian television soap *Neighbours*, **Francis Bell** was the British-born actor and later New Zealand resident who's other television credits include *Sons and Daughters* and *The Sullivans*; born in 1944, he died in 1994.

Born in 1963, **Geoff Bell** is the English actor whose many film credits include the 2003 *Girl with a Pearl Earring*, the 2008 *Freebird*, the 2011 *Mike Bassett: England Manager*, the 2011 *War Horse* and, from 2012, *Comes a Bright Day*.

Born in 1986 in Billingham, Co. Durham, Andrew James Matfin Bell is the actor better known as **Jamie Bell**. Winner of a number of awards that include a BAFTA for Best Actor in a Leading Role for his role of ballet dancer *Billy Elliot* in the 2000 true-life film of that name and a former member of the National Youth Music Theatre, he has also starred in other films that include the 2008 *Jumper* and, from 2011, *The Adventures of Tintin*.

With a Scottish father and an Iranian mother, **Catherine Bell**, born in London in 1968 and who moved to the United States when she was aged two, is the actress whose best known role, from 1997 to 2005, was that of Lieutenant Colonel Sarah Mackenzie in the television serious *JAG*.

Particularly known for his roles in a number of popular British television series and dramas that include *Shameless*, *Buried*, *Murphy's Law*, *The Bill*, *Casualty*, *Downton Abbey* and *Coronation Street*, **Neil Bell** is the English actor born in 1969 in Oldham, Lancashire.

His big screen credits include the 2002 *24 Hour Party People* and, from 2004, *Dead Man's Shoes*.

Not only an American actress but also a writer and director, **Lake Bell** was born in 1979 in New York City.

Bell 25

Television acting credits include *The Practice*, *Boston Legal* and *How to Make It in America*, while she also wrote and directed the 2003 film *In a Word…*

Bearers of the Bell name have also excelled in the highly competitive world of sport.

Nicknamed "King of the Kippax" – after the Kippax Street stand of Manchester City's Etihad Stadium – and also "Nijinsky", after the racehorse of the name that was renowned for its stamina, **Colin Bell** is the former footballer born in 1946 in Hesleden, Co. Durham.

Playing for Manchester City from 1966 to 1979, he is regarded as the club's greatest ever player, and the stadium's Bell Stand is named in his honour.

Also having played for England from 1966 to 1979, his many awards and honours include induction into the English Football Hall of Fame and an MBE for his services to the community of Manchester.

Born in Dumfries in 1986, Cameron Bell, better known as **Cammy Bell**, is the Scottish goalkeeper who has played for teams that include Queen of the South, Kilmarnock and Rangers and who was first capped for Scotland in 2010.

Born in 1937 in Johnstone, Renfrewshire, William John Bell, better known as **Willie Bell**, is the

26 *On the world stage*

Scottish former left back and manager who played in the Scottish Football League for Queens Park and twice represented his nation at international level.

In the English Football League, he played more than 200 games in the 1960s for Leeds United and also played for Leicester City and Brighton and Hove Albion. Manager for a time of Birmingham City and Lincoln City, he later moved to the United States.

Now an ordained minister, both he and his wife, Mary, founded a ministry that visits prisons in both the United States and Britain.

On the rugby pitch, **Duncan Bell**, born in 1974 in King's Lynn, Norfolk, is the English rugby union prop who has played for Bath Rugby and who has also won five caps playing as an England international.

From rugby to the high-speed sport of motor racing, **Derek Bell** is the British former racing driver who not only won the 24 Hours of Le Mans five times, and the Daytona 24 three times, but also the World Sportscar Championship twice.

Born in 1941 in Pinner, Middlesex, and also having raced in Formula One and the recipient of an OBE, he is the father of the driver **Justin Bell** – born in 1968 in Rustington, Essex, and winner of the 24

Bell 27

Hours of Le Mans in 1998, and now host of a number of motorsport related television programmes.

Playing an important role behind the scenes of Formula One, Robert Bell, better known as **Bob Bell**, was born in 1958 in Belfast.

A qualified aeronautical engineer, he has worked for teams that include McLaren, Benetton and Renault, while in 2011 he was appointed technical director of the Mercedes Formula One team.

From motor racing to athletics, **Earl H. Bell**, born in 1955 is the American pole vaulter who held the world record for a time in 1976.

Winner of the bronze medal at the 1984 Olympics, he is an inductee of America's National Track and Field Hall of Fame.

From sport to music, **Maggie Bell**, born in 1945 in Maryhill, Glasgow, is the veteran Scottish rock vocalist who, in addition to having played with the band Stone the Crows, has also enjoyed a successful solo career with albums that include her 1973 *Queen of the Night*.

In 1990, she also appeared in an episode of the popular Glasgow-based detective drama series *Taggart* – a series in which she sang its theme song, *No Mean City*.

28 *On the world stage*

Another famed female vocalist is **Madeline Bell**, born in 1942 in Newark, New Jersey.

In addition to providing backing vocals for artists who include Rod Stewart and Elton John, she also enjoyed success with the band Blue Mink with top-selling hits that include *Melting Pot*, *Banner Man* and *Good Morning Freedom*.

Born in 1964 in Peterborough, **Andy Bell** is the lead singer with the British synth-pop duo Erasure, while Marc Steven Bell, born in 1952 and better known as **Marky Ramone**, was the drummer for fifteen years with the New York-based punk band the Ramones.

Born in Toronto in 1946, **Richard Bell** was the Canadian musician who, in addition to playing piano for American rock singer Janis Joplin and her Full Tilt Boogie Band, was also a keyboardist during the 1990s for The Band; the son of the Canadian composer and musician Dr Leslie Bell, he died in 2007.

A bass guitarist for a time with British band Oasis, **Andy Bell**, born in Cardiff in 1970, left the band in 2009 along with founding member Noel Gallagher to form the band Beady Eye – following an argument between Gallagher and his brother and fellow Oasis founding member Liam.

Bell

From music to the equally creative world of the written word, **William E. Bell** is a leading Canadian author of young adult fiction.

Born in 1945, the award-winning author's books include his 1986 *Crabbe*, the 2002 *Stones* and, from 2011, *Fanatics*.

Born in 1871 in Hillhead, Glasgow, John Joy Bell, better known as **J.J. Bell**, was the Scottish journalist and author best known for his creation of the character 'Wee Macgreegor' (MacGregor) for a series of articles for the *Glasgow Evening Times*.

The popular articles, written mainly in the Glasgow vernacular, humorously described the lives of working class Glaswegians.

He died in 1934, while his equally popular books include the 1902 *Wee MacGreegor*, the 1904 *Wullie McWattie's Master* and his 1931 *Laird of Glenlaggan*.

In the world of public relations, Timothy John Leigh Bell, better known as **Tim Bell**, is the British advertising and public relations executive best known for the role he played in helping to secure General Election victories for the late Conservative Prime Minister Margaret Thatcher.

Born in 1941, his first job was as a post boy

for ABC Television – but later entering the world of advertising and public relations he helped to found the firm of Saatchi and Saatchi, in 1970, before founding Lowe Howard Spink & Bell in 1985.

In Margaret Thatcher's first election victory in 1979, it was Bell who created the "Labour isn't Working" campaign slogan, while he also advised her on everything from interview techniques to hairstyle.

Knighted in 1990, he was further ennobled by being made a life peer eight years later as Baron Bell of Belgravia.

One particularly noted family of the Bell name is one that includes the first compiler of *The Times* crossword, a former war reporter and politician and a distinguished translator of a number of literary works.

Born in London in 1901, **Adrian Bell** was aged 19 when he decided to embark on a career in agriculture and, leaving the smoke of the city behind, settled in rural Suffolk.

He farmed at a number of locations over the following decades, including at a small-holding at Redisham, near Beccles.

His experiences as a farmer led to him penning a number of best-selling books on the

Bell 31

countryside, including his 1930 *Corduroy*, the 1931 *Silver Ley* and, in 1932, *The Cherry Tree* – all later published as a trilogy in 1940.

By the late 1920s, *The Times* had started losing circulation to its rival the *Daily Telegraph*, in part due to the fact that the latter ran a popular daily crossword.

Bell's father, a *Times* journalist, recommended his son to the editor as a crossword 'setter' – despite the fact that he had never even solved one let alone set one before. Nevertheless, he was taken on and his first crossword published on January 2, 1930.

From then until 1978, he set thousands of puzzles and is recognised as having helped to establish the newspaper's distinctive cryptic clue style.

The author of further books that include his 1942 *Apple Acre*, the 1946 *The Budding Morrow* and his 1961 autobiographical *My Own Master*, he died in 1980.

He was the father of the former radio and television war reporter and Member of Parliament **Martin Bell**.

Born in 1938 in the family small-holding at Redisham, he joined the BBC as a reporter in Norwich in 1962, later moving to London and becoming a BBC foreign affairs correspondent.

He covered a number of conflicts over the next thirty years, including Vietnam and Angola and, frequently dressed for camera in his 'trademark' white jacket, the war in Bosnia – where he was severely wounded by shrapnel in 1992.

Leaving the BBC to stand as an independent candidate in the 1997 General Election, he won the Tatton seat in Cheshire, where the sitting Conservative MP Neil Hamilton had become involved in allegations of 'sleaze'; he held the seat until 2001.

The recipient of a number of honours and awards that include an OBE and two Royal Television Society Reporter of the Year awards, he now acts as an ambassador for UNICEF.

He is the brother of **Anthea Bell**, born in 1936, noted not only for her translations of literary works but also, along with co-translator Derek Hockridge, the French *Asterix* comics; she is also the recipient of a number of honours and awards that include an OBE for services to literature and literary translation.